WHAT TO DO WHEN YOUR RIGHT ARM FALLS OFF

A Survival Guide for Widows

Susenne Telage

ISBN 978-1-0980-7895-9 (paperback)
ISBN 978-1-0980-8532-2 (hardcover)
ISBN 978-1-0980-7896-6 (digital)

Copyright © 2021 by Susenne Telage

All rights reserved. No part of this publication may be reproduced, distributed, or transmitted in any form or by any means, including photocopying, recording, or other electronic or mechanical methods without the prior written permission of the publisher. For permission requests, solicit the publisher via the address below.

Christian Faith Publishing, Inc.
832 Park Avenue
Meadville, PA 16335
www.christianfaithpublishing.com

Printed in the United States of America

This book is dedicated to Bob and to my beautiful daughters who have always been extraordinary blessings and my best friends.

The pen and ink drawings are created by my sixteen-year-old granddaughter, Kate Marie.

Cover illustration by Susenne Telage

The Tsunami

Losing a loved one is like a tsunami…
it is a massive force of nature that comes (often without warning) Knocks you down, turns your world upside down and destroys everything in its path and its waves keep coming and coming. The waves get less destructive and are farther and farther apart with time.

You can survive.
Keep your head up.
Keep breathing.

Dear Readers,

I am writing this book for all of my sisters, little sisters and big sisters, who are going through the same rite of passage, the trail of tears called widowhood. When one loses a spouse, she walks through a curtain of uncertainty into territory unlike anywhere she has been before. Not only does she discover a great dark void, but she is then assaulted from every direction by unexpected monsters and ghosts... mental, physical, and spiritual weakness, guilt, regret and confusion to name a few. They don't tell you about this at the hospital, in church or at the grief classes. If they did, it didn't register, so I am writing this to help guide you through the maze.

When you lose a partner, your best friend, your lover, the breadwinner, the tire changer, father of your children, the man you were going to grow old with, it is like an amputation and you must learn how to do tasks with one hand that were formerly accomplished by two.

You will now decide when the car needs new tires and what size they are, what you have to gather together to pay taxes, transfer bills, and credit cards and who can do the taxes, who's going to protect you when you hear night noises, how does ONE know how and when to wrap pipes for a hard freeze and on and on and on.

Step by step, holding God's hand. That's how I did it.

Blessings,
S

The One-Year Fog

When my husband was dying in the hospital, it was a series of events almost too hideous to endure. I keep all the details of those last days together locked away. I do all that I can to keep that time and those memories hidden. Each widow may have her own torturous memories. There is no need to recount mine. "Don't look back...that's not the direction in which you're moving." Each detail is painfully crystal clear if I do choose to dredge them up to consciousness, but the curious thing is that after the gory battle there is a quiet void, a thick fog that settled over my life.

I don't remember exactly which steps I had to take to resume living a normal life. I do know that the fog was debilitating. Logic was not logical. Amnesia was a constant state and weakness manifested itself mentally, physically, and emotionally.

I also experienced a state of inertia that was so curious, finding it next to impossible to get out of bed, out of a chair and on to the next activity. My inner voice was like a tough drill sergeant, "Get up, lady! Move your ass! C'mon, you can do it…stand up! Move on!"

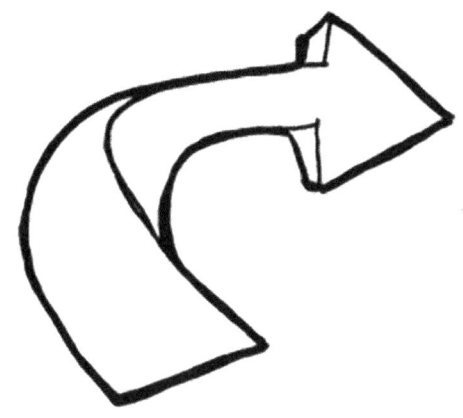

New Chapter Changes

Why write?

Thoughts are slipping in and out of my mind distorted like a Dali dripping clock.

Temporarily, I will leave my career as an artist and I will write, laying my thoughts and imagination down on paper. I feel compelled to do so. I want to help a weeping widow. Also, swapping my always in disarray studio for a serene and neat writing environment has great appeal.

Streamlining is good. This is a good time for changing habits and trying new things. Ask God to lead you, and He will usher you to changes in this new chapter of your life. Here are some of my new chapter changes:

Volunteering:

I signed up to work on a career transition ministry.

Bible studies: A wonderful way to meet like-minded friends and get to know God better.

Taking big bubble baths at 3 a.m. if you feel like it. Your time is your own now.

Binge watch a TV series…indulge yourself in little non-fattening pleasures.

Go on vacations with children and grandchildren and friends.

Learn another language or study the Stoic Philosophy.

More dinners out with friends

Join a book club: Listening to books in Audible is like someone reading a bedtime story to you. (Don't forget to set the sleep-timer zzzzz).

Take the Grandies out on dates. One-on-one is a superb way to grow closer to each of them.

I have found that filling up my cup of life is a thirst quencher for sorrow.

The Quality of Mercy

I have never been one who dealt with illness very well. In myself, I was in denial.

When I encountered illness in others, I just wanted to use that line from *Moonstruck*, "Snap out of it!"

My quality of mercy was strained.

"The Cruel War Is Raging," that Joan Baez folk song was one of our favorites. Bob and I used to sing it together and even accompanied it on our guitars when we were younger. It would always impress the children and now I sing it again in my head. A mournful song about a woman who does not want to see her love leave her to go off to war; she begs to go with him and he constantly says no. Then she says, "I'll tie back my hair, men's clothing I'll put on, I'll pass as your comrade as we march along." And the song has a happy ending when he relents and says yes, but that doesn't happen to me.

My love has gone off, had to fight the cruel war of cancer, lost and I am left alone to do battle with grief.

My love was not seriously ill for long. He dealt with the chemo like a trouper until the fourth round which was so hard on his system that he spiraled tragically into death within weeks. How many weeks I can't say. From the time during Lent when he fell in our hallway three times (making me think of Christ carrying his cross) until his tragic end on April 4, 2016, and on until at least a year later, I was in a very thick fog mentally, emotionally, and physically.

The Storm

    I have learned and overcome so much on this grief journey.

    We were a great team, always ready for a new adventure. He was in business development for the oil and gas industry. Bob was someone who valued everyone he met and people gravitated to his sincere acceptance and to his wonderful sense of humor. He was devoted to family and generous beyond measure. He served on several boards. We entertained many clients, golfed, and traveled pretty extensively. We adored our daughters and our sons-in-law and cherished our six grandchildren. Life was glamorous and exciting. We had our off moments but for the most part, truly lived the good life together.

Then he was gone.

I waited for the recommended one year, then gave up the dream home we had just designed. It was in a golf club community enhanced by a huge landscaped yard, five bedrooms, and beautiful furnishings and I moved into a three-bedroom apartment, which I must say, was so attractive with its Parisian feel, that the move was not terribly painful and it was great to shed all of the responsibility home ownership. I was excited about that chapter. Now I have moved into two rooms in my daughter's house—again a chapter I was looking forward to but one that entailed more challenges than I had anticipated. The move was harder this time because I had to say a final goodbye to so much of my past. I had to have the generosity and courage to give away furnishings and souvenirs and belongings that were part of my happy life with Bob. Getting to know so many Venezuelan refugees (who needed everything!) helped me with the purging, but it was still painful to watch half of my material life disappear.

I'm seventy-eight years old and have been a widow for over four years. I am just beginning to realize once again how beautiful life is and so decided I should write this book to help my widowed sisters to negotiate this very rocky, difficult journey of loss. Many things happened to me that were unexpected, and I would like to help other widows to make some sense of the changes.

From My Diary

I kept a diary from the beginning of this dark journey and realize on the re-reading that there were so many moments of light along the way. As I've expressed earlier, the bleak and wretched moments will help no one, so I will not go into any detail on those but will recount my silver linings on the dark storm clouds.

Entry January 2, 2016

Coincidently it is 2016. I have saved this book (Royal Opera House Diary) since 1988 and this year the dates are correct... Time has converged to keep this book current. I've kept it for the lovely illustrations, but when I decided to start a diary, I found this and decided to use it.

Description of two heart stents and a bile duct surgery and discovery of a tumor.

He was released in time to celebrate a beautiful Christmas with the family. The girls have been more compassionate and more devoted to him than we could ever have imagined... so attentive, concerned, and totally engaged. God truly blessed us with the most amazing daughters!

Description of the agonizing medical maze we are struggling to get through.

Each time, we see an impossible situation, we experience the power of God working for us. The whole family is joined together in a solidarity of hope. Tara has worked tirelessly to wade through the legalities of the situation. Tia has been a constant encourager. All are praying continuously.

Father T says a spontaneous beautiful healing service for Bob after Mass. We cling to hope.

Description of the myriad of medical roadblocks and new terrifying discoveries and reports.

Entry January 28, 2016

Since Medicare has failed us we have taken advantage of D & S's generosity (who paid cash) and have gone to a highly recommended physician who has developed an aggressive plan to do battle with the cancer devastating Bob's body. Dr. C told us every part of the plan and every scenario yesterday, adding "It is in God's hands." It is indeed.

Entry Sunday, January 31 2016

We are not going to Mass...afraid of the germs. The girls brought groceries and dinner last night. We sat in every other chair in the dining room...so much has been taken away.

How lovely it is to see the family's generosity, love, and devotion. David made the most exquisite card full of beauty and love. Todd pours his heart out in compassion. The Grandies all pray earnest pure children's prayers. Della prayed that when things are the hardest, we can see God's power and love more clearly...out of the mouths of babes!

Entry February 8, 2016

Still no evidence of help arriving from Medicare.

The Holy Spirit revealed something to me, whenever I look up at the crucifix, I am reminded of the hideous sacrifice Jesus made to forgive my sins, but lately something else jumps out at me: Jesus's poor skinned knees, bleeding, humiliating for the King of kings!

Yesterday, I succumbed to weakness and begin crying at the unfairness and difficulty of it all. Later, I felt like such a weak failure. Now I know that when my cross causes me to fall, he will be there to help me carry the burden. Thank you, God.

February 24, 2016

Bob is completing the second chemotherapy session this week.

Entry March 20, 2016

Bob has completed three rounds of chemo and goes back tomorrow for the fourth round.

The past week and a half have been very disheartening. I pray that he has the strength to survive his survival.

Good Friday, March 24, 2016

Bob fell down three times. We called 911.

Entry April 2, 2016

March has come and gone. Bob has spiraled downhill quickly...or perhaps uphill to God's hands.

Entry April 4, 2016

We are all in CCU saying goodbye and sobbing with grief. Friends and family have come to our aid to help us fight our way through this storm.
9:30 a.m.
It is done.

Entry November 6, 2016

The fog is beginning to lift on rare occasions. What a gloomy and treacherous path I am trudging through. Punctuated, I must say, with glimpses of light and lots of amazing grace and love but nevertheless a dark night.

Glancing back, I recall the days when Bob left us.

Tia, Tara, and I took all six Grandies to Tara's house. We gathered them together and explained as gently as we could that their beloved Bibby had died. We all cried together and prayed and hugged. So many tears!

One of the older children could not cry and the youngest seemed to truly celebrate the fact that's his Bibby was in the very happiest place. Each of us dealt individually with their own GRIEF.

We had a quiet beautiful mass for just the family at one of the painted churches in the country (later David would tell us that, during the service he saw "a fade" of Bibby in the church all dressed up and smiling)...curious.

We went to our home afterward where neighbors had prepared a beautiful meal for us. Bob's siblings, niece, and nephew had all flown in and we gathered the family together and we spent the evening reminiscing about Bob's kindness, quirks, accomplishments, his love, and his life.

Making funeral arrangements was such an ordeal, but the family did it together and there truly is strength in numbers because we all supported and comforted each other through the awkward and confusing decision making.

Memorial Service

We had an awesome memorial service that was a spectacular tribute to Bob. Every member of the family had a special part in the service.

The girls and I stood at the doors of the mortuary and greeted the standing-room-only throng of people who came to say good-bye. The Holy Spirit was with me because I remembered names from fifty-plus years of friends, acquaintances, and coworkers. I was so touched by their love and compassion.

I told everyone in the family that they could say a few words at the service if they wished to. Some could not and I totally understood. I was surprised when eight-year-old David told me that he wanted to speak.

"There will be a microphone and many people there," I said.

"Yes, I want to do that," he replied.

I put him last so that he could watch and be comfortable with the situation. The girls and I each spoke, then Bob's sister and brother. All were eloquent loving memorials. Most everyone was crying. We had a slide show of Bob's life that, mysteriously (miraculously), was in total sync with the reminiscing. David was the last. He told a humorous story that made everyone chuckle. He then said, "If you will bow your heads, let's pray together for my Bibby followed by a perfect prayer." There was not one dry eye in the room! "And a little child shall lead them."

The burial was a short walk away but for me a lifetime journey. I knew in my heart that my beloved husband of fifty-one years was gone. I don't go to graves, I never have believed there was any purpose in that, but that day I had to be with my family and recognize Bob's end on this earth… Horrible!

On the way home, there was a beautiful rainbow over where Bob was buried. Since that day, I have seen many, especially on special family occasions. I accept each one as a sign of promise and presence…the promise of hope and the presence of God.

WHAT TO DO WHEN YOUR RIGHT ARM FALLS OFF

Many times, on a variety of special occasions, we have seen another curious sight: a large white plane with lights blazing. Bob was the most loyal and proud frequent flyer on this planet, and this would be his sign of personal choice. The first time the plane appeared was the afternoon that we gathered the children together to tell them of his death. We had all gone out to the back yard afterward, and on that sunny sad afternoon, the white plane roared by, lights blazing. Another time was when my daughter and I left her doctor's office, nearly skipping down the parking lot because of a great diagnosis. Another time, it flew by on a mountain at a family gathering, another time when we all gathered together to serve the homeless. It is curious.

Another sign is a bright blue flash that emanates from my wedding ring on special occasions. The last time being when we were at U of H to honor Bob with the Endowment Scholarship in his name (created by one of the boards that he had served on). One day, I was looking out at the view from my patio, thinking, *Now the signs are few and far between. Is it just my imagination that God gives me signs?*

When I looked up, much to my amazement, there was a circular rainbow around the sun. When I photographed the wonder, a bright blue spot appeared in a different position in every photograph.

His children feel Bob's presence, his sister does on the golf course, and friends have said that they do. I do not really feel his presence with the exception of one very vivid dream in which he appeared in a pale blue shirt with a great tan and a glowing smile. I awoke feeling blissfully happy at the thought of his well-being. Only because of divine reassurance am I at peace.

Guilt is a favorite tool of the evil one. One day, I was agonizing over what more I should have or could have done: been more patient, fed him better, golfed with him more etc. When I received this clear message:

>"It was not in your hands.
>It was not in the physician's hands.
>It was in my hands and my plan is perfect."

I accept that truth.

Another reassurance came when I listened to the biblical story of the friends who lowered their crippled companion down through the roof in hopes that Jesus would heal him. I had prayed for the miracle of healing so hard.

Why not a miracle for us? I thought. *Jesus healed that crippled man, why not Bob?* then the words Jesus said hit me like a bolt of light: "Pick up your mat and go home."

Bob was home.

In the days following Bob's passing, I dealt with a full range of emotions. My goddaughter niece had a magnificent wedding in Boston in June. One of the things that I had said to Bob in that last month was "Please stay strong. You've got to get better. I don't want to go to the wedding alone," but I did.

The girls and I had a High Tea for the bride at the Boston Public Library. Such a lovely event! When all around me was beautiful and happy, inside of me everything felt unreal and impossible. It was all I could do to "keep calm and carry on." I fell down at the reception. My muscles were so weak!

Entry August 14, 2017

Much time has passed since my last entry. I have gone to yet another family wedding (his side) and have survived the emotional pain of the void that is. But I stayed upright this time!

I've moved on literally and with much difficulty. I have sold our dream home. I moved into a beautiful apartment. It is like a five-star resort complete with so many amenities: swimming pool, social room, library, fitness center, and a beautiful shopping center for a backyard. Coincidentally, I spent my first night there on our anniversary; is Bob still able to work deals for me in his afterlife?

The grief tsunami waves keep coming unexpectedly. Some of them knock me down, like seeing his signature on the safe deposit box document and some just shake my balance like ordering a pica colada poolside. Things we did together are brought into clear and painful focus continually. I know I cannot be in denial about the loss, but I also know that I must move into the next strange chapter of my life for my own sake and that of my family.

From the day of his death until now, I have been aware of the fact that I am setting an example of how to deal with death for my family. What I do and how I behave will perhaps be a template for them one day.

I do sense a spiritual battle very acutely. The evil one loves to drape me in sorrow, guilt, and regret. It feels like a heavy wool coat drenched with tears. The dampness and weight is oppressive...no comfort from cold, no protection and no warmth. I am awakened each morning with the knowledge that I am on my own. I feel a little lost on this new lonesome pathway.

April 14, 2018

The months have sped by, and today is Bob's birthday. Now there are fewer waves of sorrow and they are becoming less intense. When they come, they take me by surprise: I break down and cry when I'm talking to my son-in-law about getting new tires, or when mail arrives with Bob's name on it, or when we have a family celebration and he is not there, or when I awaken in the morning to realize that he's not in bed with me and never will be again. Each is a thorn that I offer up as a prayer.

I am growing stronger spiritually, finding purpose in my life. I count the blessings: time to devote to my family, guilt-free time to help my girls and grandies, unrestricted time, quiet time to listen for God's messages to me.

I have new freedoms now: freedom to move to the cadence of my own drumbeat... not under obligation to please, compromise, or share. Don't get me wrong, I would trade any of these new freedoms for another chance to be with Bob, but I do not have that choice so I will count the freedoms as blessings and be grateful.

I'm filling my life to the brim with activity, crowding out the grief. Family, art classes, and a new ministry (another of God's surprising answers to my prayers). I have no desire to date, but I do miss being in the company of men. Bob had taken me to client dinners, conventions, and meetings. I like the way men think, laugh, and generally behave and I miss that in my life. These days I find myself surrounded only by women and children on the survival lifeboat. I do love them but crave the diversity of being with both genders. In my restlessness, I knew I needed to do something worthwhile like volunteer work in my new church. When I called, I was told that there was a need for more help in the Career Transition Ministry. It is a program created to assist the unemployed, underemployed, or those in career transition to sharpen skills and take powerful steps on their road to successful employment. I volunteered to help in any way that I could, thinking that I could be a greeter, make name tags, etc. I have always been self-employed and have never interviewed for a job, so I had no expertise that area, but I certainly was in career transition myself...fifty-one years of being a wife had ended, and I was learning to pick up the pieces and move on. Also, I hope that I helped Bob get through the three or four times he himself was out of work, so I did have that experience to offer plus the desire to help others get through a difficult time. Much to my surprise, I ended up being the only woman on the team. God has given me that time with men that I was missing.

    The ministry has taught me so much: as we have provided a safe haven and help for shaken egos and confused hearts, the mentoring has done great healing work for me. I've met so many beautiful people (many Venezuelan refugees). My life is being enriched.

August 15, 2019

God's favor is so surprising!

Time is flying by. The children are all getting ready to go back to school, growing up so fast. What a brief span of time from freckles to liver spots.

The Great Eleven-Year-Old Adventure

When I was eleven years old, my grandmother took me on a trail ride in the Colorado Rockies. The oldest of five children, I relished this grand solo adventure. My grandmother ran the trail rides and gave me a roommate who did not speak any English. The two of us managed to communicate beautifully with charades and much laughter. It was the first time I was really on my own. It was a turning point in my young life. Years later, when I knew that I was to have grandchildren, I made a vow that I would take each one of them on their own Great Eleven-Year-Old Adventure.

Bob and I had taken five such amazing trips. The destination was a surprise revealed to each one at the airport. What fun! Now the last of the grandchildren was to turn eleven, and I would have to make all arrangements on my own. I decided that a cruise would be the safest most hassle-free adventure. We sailed out of Galveston for a week long journey to Mexico, Aruba, and Jamaica. What a glorious time we had! I treasure each moment of that trip: dressing for dinners, sculptured towels, being rocked to sleep by the waves, all of the shipboard activities, making new friends, the port tours, beautiful beaches, amazing sunsets, swimming with dolphins, island music, Jamaican jerky on Thanksgiving instead of turkey...so much fun! I hope it was as meaningful for my eleven-year-old buddy as it was for me!

New Arrangements

When I started thinking about my life and the last three years as a widow, I decided that I should make new living arrangements. My youngest daughter is a single mom with three teenagers and two businesses. She has so much on her plate, part of which includes a lot of business travel. I came to her with the idea that we could live together, and I would be there when she was out of town. I have watched two precious people in one of my Bible studies do this and admired their giving spirits. My daughter went overboard in generosity as always and purchased a really beautiful home for the five of us. I have a separate suite with its own private entrance. I must say that there were some adjustments that we all had to make in the beginning, but now, nearly a year later, it has turned out to be a win-win situation.

Currently, I am in the middle of a self-imposed quarantine, as the world is plagued with the coronavirus. Everything has stopped. Restaurants, churches, schools, and all non-essential businesses are ordered closed and on April 1 there is a stay-at-home order for another month (no April Fool's joke). I've already been quarantined for three weeks. People are staying home with their families and rethinking their daily routines. We are staying six feet away from one another, but we've painted together, learned to crochet, cooked, built an above-ground-garden, had dinners together, caught up on news with friends and relatives, played poker, done jigsaw puzzles...gone back to the basics of civilized living. It is my belief that God has given the world a big time out...sent us all to our rooms to think about our lives! Sadly, there are also many deaths and I wonder if these are the beginning of the end times?

Sometimes, I feel as if I'm imprisoned in a self-centered world. When one suddenly becomes so involved in weathering the solo storm, being concerned with how and why to manage living, it is easy to fall into a pattern of self-involvement that is both lonely and counterproductive.

The best escape from this prison, that I have discovered, is service to others. Real satisfaction comes when we truly care about and can be a helping hand to someone. Prayer and service are my biggest healing suggestions.

God has helped me weather the storms of life over and over again.

I sometimes call out to him and yearn to hear His voice. He speaks in so many ways: often through others who offer wisdom that "jumps out at me" with such clarity that it cannot be overlooked.

He sometimes speaks when we look at events and, in retrospect, realize that only the hand of God could have orchestrated such perfection. God's creation testifies to His genius and to His glory. His sunsets are so awesome…a heavenly good night kiss!

As I write this, the voice of God guides my thinking. Often, especially when raising children I've spoken with wisdom that does not come from my brilliance but was truly inspired by the Holy Spirit. This is my constant prayer: "Breathe in me, Holy Spirit, that I might be holy."

Listen

We cannot hear the voice of God unless we give Him our rapt attention.

"Be still and know that I Am God" (Psalm 46:10).

God is royalty, and we must honor Him by waiting for Him, trusting him, and paying respect to Him by the way we live. We widows were mentioned often in the Bible and the messages instruct all to care for us lovingly. Why would God tell others to do so if He Himself did not cherish us and tenderly care for our every need?
"Jesus, I trust in you."
"They" will tell you, my dear widow, that there are several stages of grief: denial, anger, bargaining, depression, and acceptance. I have experienced each of those stages, but perhaps not in the ways one might imagine. I have denied that this could happen to me. I've never

been angry at God but seeing a commercial for a river cruise (our next planned adventure) has made me shout out the F word...shockingly not my style! I tried bargaining during every moment of those last days. Depression at its lowest point took the form of really not caring about anything at all. Weeping and wailing would have been easier! And finally acceptance. I no longer look at an older couple holding hands with envy or bitterness. I have finally relinquished my perceived control and come to the realization that all is well.

Having laid out my experiences I now have second thoughts. Is this retelling of my tragedy nothing more than self-indulgent DIY therapy? That is not the intent I assure you. I mean for this guide to help you negotiate your way through the confusion and hurt of the grief maze. I think that retelling my experiences might help you to identify with some of the challenges and to realize that you certainly are not alone in your sorrow nor in the way that you deal with it. My experiences will not be yours and the way we cope will be vastly different, but there is a common thread of suffering that can be endured and a hope that can be achieved. You are not alone, though I know that's how you're feeling sometimes. There is light at the end of this tunnel and the darkness on occasion will amplify the incredibly beautiful light of God. You do have access to His comfort and wisdom. Eventually, you will be able to greet new days with hope and joy. You will laugh and celebrate life again. You will learn to tuck away precious memories deep in your heart and be grateful for each of them. Treasure them forever. Be patient and trust.

    I have experienced so many peaks and valleys in these last four years. I am a happy lady who has learned better how to live in the moment. I'm regaining use of that missing right arm. The amputation has made me stronger, gentler, and calmer in many ways.

Love,
S

Self-Reflections

Now that I have recorded my thoughts, I have to tell you that is has helped me to discover progress that I've made and is a good roadmap telling me where I have been, am now, and where I am going.

You are the best sounding board for your own personal grief. I've discovered that, for me, sharing it with others just is counterproductive.

Your sorrow hurts your children and friends and is an added burden for others getting through a period of grieving.

Having a trusted therapist or spiritual advisor is a gift, but if that is not the case, I strongly recommend journaling.

Here are a few thoughts to start:

What kind of person do I want to be?

What is my dream environment?

As my wounds are beginning to heal,
I feel your presence when...

Do I find time each day for gratitude?

I remember how much we laughed when…

Is there someone I could help?

What subject fascinates me?

Who do I admire? Why?

How can I begin to live more in the present?

What is my dearest possession?

The Bible says "fear not" 365 times!

Do I meditate at least once a week?

What can this adversity teach me?

Have I recorded our marriage, joys, travels, etc. A photo book is fun to create and will be a treasured keepsake.

Other ideas:

Take a watercolor course.

Do you know that on your phone, you have the whole Bible (Laudate)?

Wise advice on a myriad of subjects (YouTube).

Mental exercises (Lumosity).

On-line courses galore!

Volunteer opportunities for every area.

Remember: life is about the elaborate power of God's love.

Essential to worship: less of me, more of Thee.

Laugh at yourself.

Sign up for a new interest group.

Create a really pleasant sanctuary for yourself.

Write letters.

Do spring cleaning even if it's winter.

Relax and be grateful for each new insight.

Jesus said, "I have come that you might have life and have it to the full" (John 10:10).

About the Author

Susenne Telage is an artist, writer and author of a new book, *What to Do When Your Right Arm Falls Off: A Widow's Survival Guide.*

She has written and illustrated children's books and is a professional artist in Houston, Texas.

She is a woman of faith and takes great delight in sharing her spiritual journey with her children, six grandchildren, and in Bible studies and faith instruction. A world traveler and lifelong learner, Susenne has been a ski patrolman, restaurant owner, advertising agency president, and a gallery owner. These diverse experiences give her a unique view of life.

CPSIA information can be obtained
at www.ICGtesting.com
Printed in the USA
LVHW071543260721
693699LV00019B/695

9 781098 078959